P9-AEX-637

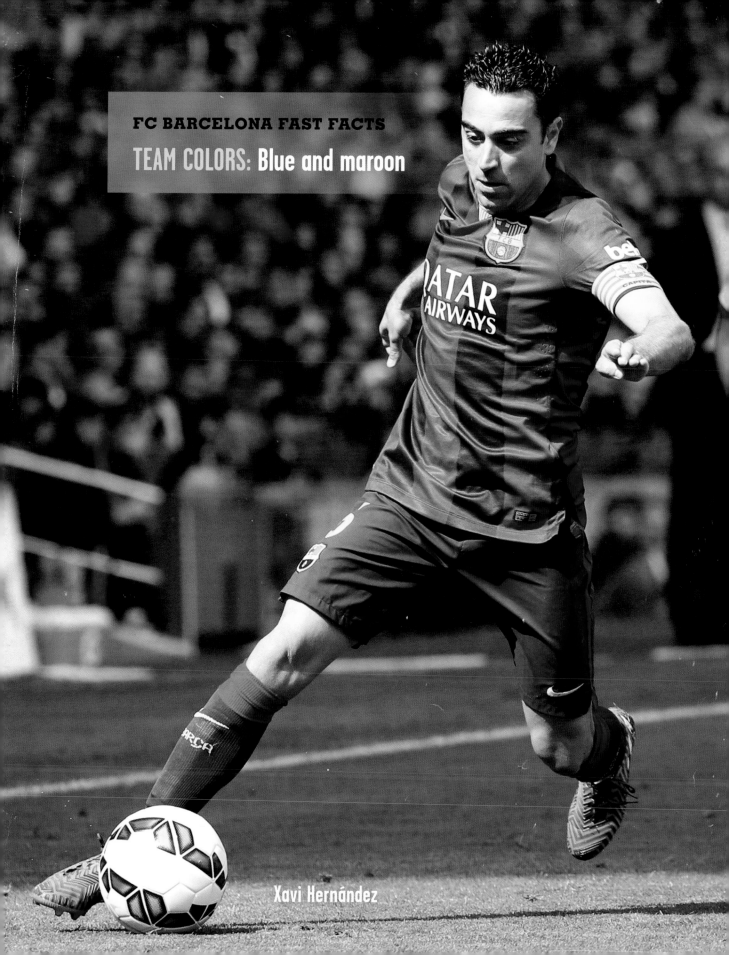

FC BARCELONA FAST FACTS

TEAM COLORS: Blue and maroon

Xavi Hernández

Published by **Creative Education** and **Creative Paperbacks**
P.O. Box 227, Mankato, Minnesota 56002
Creative Education and Creative Paperbacks are imprints of
The Creative Company
www.thecreativecompany.us

Design and production by **Christine Vanderbeek**
Art direction by **Rita Marshall**
Printed in the United States of America

Photographs by Alamy (MARKA), Corbis (Christian Liewig/TempSport,
Daniel Ochoa De Olza/AP, GERRY PENNY/epa, Splash News/Splash News,
MIKEL TRIGUEROS/URBANANDSPORT/CORDON PRESS/Cordon Press,
Joan Valls/NurPhoto), Creative Commons Wikimedia (Weidenfild and
Nicolson), Getty Images (PIERRE-PHILIPPE MARCOU, STAFF, Bob Thomas),
photosinbox.com, Shutterstock (anat chant, Natursports, tele52)

Library of Congress Cataloging-in-Publication Data
Whiting, Jim.
FC Barcelona / Jim Whiting.
p. cm. — (Soccer stars)
Includes index.
Summary: An elementary introduction to the Spanish soccer team FC
Barcelona, including a brief history since the team's 1899 founding, its
main rival, notable players, and Champions League titles.

ISBN 978-1-60818-801-7 (hardcover)
ISBN 978-1-62832-354-2 (pbk)
ISBN 978-1-56660-848-0 (eBook)
Futbol Club Barcelona—History—Juvenile literature.
GV943.6.B3 W45 2016
796.334094672—dc23   2016002063

CCSS: RI.1.1, 2, 3, 4, 5, 6, 7; RI.2.1, 2, 4, 5, 6, 7, 10; RF.1.1, 3, 4; RF.2.3, 4

First Edition HC 9 8 7 6 5 4 3 2 1
First Edition PBK 9 8 7 6 5 4 3 2 1

Right: Lionel Messi

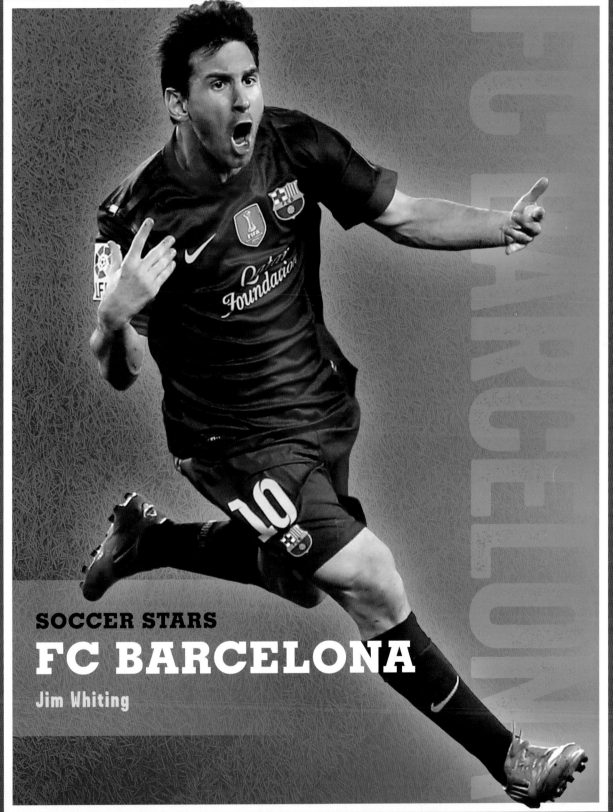

SOCCER STARS
FC BARCELONA

Jim Whiting

CREATIVE EDUCATION · CREATIVE PAPERBACKS

Dani Alves

TABLE OF CONTENTS

SOCCER STARS FC BARCELONA

FC Barcelona in 2006

Introducing FC Barcelona

FC BARCELONA is one of the best teams in Spain. It plays in La Liga, Spain's top soccer league. Barça (*BAHR-suh*) has millions of fans around the world.

HOME ARENA: Estadio del Camp Nou

Barcelona, Spain

The Capital of Catalonia

THE TEAM IS from Barcelona, Spain's second-largest city. Barcelona is also the capital of the region of Catalonia. It has its own language and government.

FC Barcelona in 1903

SOCCER STARS   PAULINO ALCÁNTARA 1912–16, 1918–27

Known for his powerful kick, Paulino had the most goals (369) in team history until 2014. He is famous for the "police goal," a shot so hard that it took both the ball and a wandering policeman into the net!

Golden Age

A YOUNG SWISS man named Hans Kamper started FC Barcelona in 1899. The team began a heated **rivalry** with Real Madrid. In the early years, Barça won most of the games between the two teams. A "golden age" began in 1919. Barça was Spain's best team for 10 years! When La Liga started in 1929, Barça won the first title.

Luis Suárez

Reviving Barcelona

SPAIN FOUGHT a **civil war** from 1936 to 1939. The team did not play well during that time. But then it rebounded in the late 1940s. Barça's 1951–52 season was one of the greatest in soccer history. The team won five major trophies!

Johan Cruyff

SOCCER STARS **JOHAN CRUYFF** 1973–78

Born in the Netherlands, attacking midfielder Johan was named European Player of the 20th Century in 1999.

Real's Reign

FOR YEARS afterward, Real Madrid played better than the *Blaugrana*. The arrival of Dutch attacking midfielder Johan Cruyff helped the team win La Liga in 1974. It was Barça's first title since 1960.

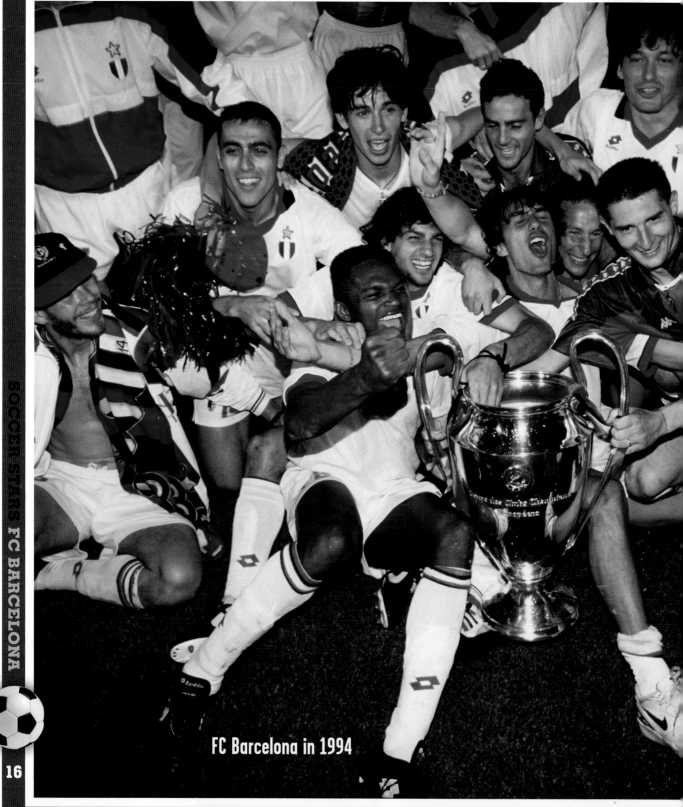

FC Barcelona in 1994

The top scorer in La Liga two years in a row, Quini was kidnapped the day before a big game. He was released, unharmed, a month later.

Return of the Dutchman

BARÇA DIDN'T WIN La Liga again for 10 years. Then Cruyff became manager in 1988. The team won four La Liga titles in eight years.

Lionel Messi

Back on Top

LIONEL MESSI JOINED the team in 2004. The superstar led Barça to **Champions League** titles in 2006, 2009, 2011, and 2015. Today, Messi and other greats such as forward Neymar Jr. help keep FC Barcelona at the top of Europe's teams.

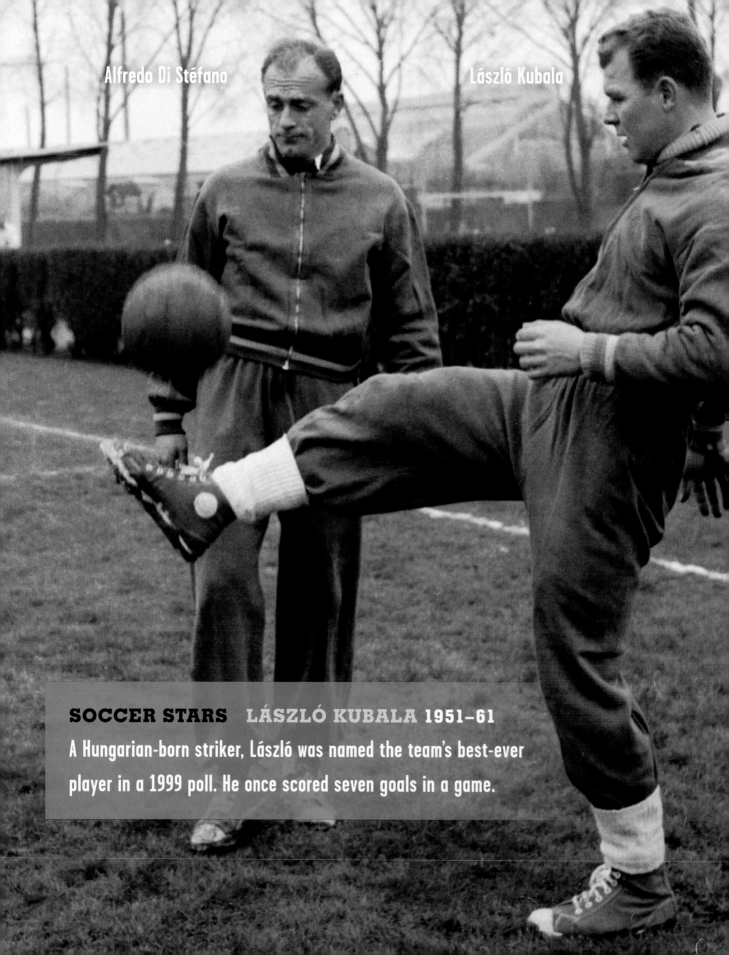

Alfredo Di Stéfano

László Kubala

SOCCER STARS **LÁSZLÓ KUBALA 1951–61**

A Hungarian-born striker, László was named the team's best-ever
player in a 1999 poll. He once scored seven goals in a game.

Champions League Titles

Year		Score
1992	FC Barcelona	1
	Sampdoria (Italy)	0
2006	FC Barcelona	2
	Arsenal (England)	1
2009	FC Barcelona	2
	Manchester United (England)	0
2011	FC Barcelona	3
	Manchester United (England)	1
2015	FC Barcelona	3
	Juventus (Italy)	1

Read More

Ejaz, Khadija. *Lionel Messi*. Hockessin, Del.: Mitchell Lane, 2014.

Jökulsson, Illugi. *FC Barcelona: More Than a Club*. New York: Abbeville Press, 2014.

Websites

BARÇA FANS
http://fans.fcbarcelona.com/?_ga=1.108317319.440510087.1442422216
Check out the team's official fan page for links to player information, videos, quizzes, and a countdown to game day.

LIONEL MESSI BIOGRAPHY
http://www.biography.com/people/lionel-messi-555732
This story of Lionel Messi includes his background, quick facts, and a video.

Glossary

Champions League an annual tournament among the top European soccer teams to see which one is best

civil war a war between two or more groups in a country

rivalry an intense competition between two teams

Note: Every effort has been made to ensure that the websites listed at left are suitable for children, that they have educational value, and that they contain no inappropriate material. However, because of the nature of the Internet, it is impossible to guarantee that these sites will remain active indefinitely or that their contents will not be altered.

Index